THE ILLUSTRATED
MOTORCYCLE LEGENDS

Norton

ROY BACON

SUNBURST BOOKS

This edition published 1996 by
Sunburst Books
Kiln House, 210 New Kings Road
London SW6 4NZ

© Text Roy Bacon 1996
© Layout and Design the Promotional Reprint Company Ltd 1996

ISBN 1 85778 219 4

ACKNOWLEDGEMENTS

The author and publishers wish to acknowledge their debt to all who loaned material and
photographs for this book. Much of this came from the Vintage Motor Cycle Club, the
Norton Owners Club and the firm itself, but others who helped were Jim Davies, the
RAC, Californian friends Paul Adams and Art Sirota, and Englishman Ian Kennedy now
living and working in Canada. A number of the pictures were from the author's files or
taken by him over the years. Our thanks to all who helped.

FRONT COVER :
Classic Norton, the first rotary-powered model for the public,
air-cooled and a limited edition of 100 machines

BACK COVER AND TITLE PAGE:
The F1 Norton Superbike in its JPS livery was
striking in looks and used advanced technology

Printed and bound in China

Contents

FOUNDATIONS 1898-1919

Norton was, and still is, one of the most respected names in the British motorcycle industry whose marque was founded in Edwardian times by James Lansdowne Norton. A deeply religious, principled man of the highest standards, he worked hard to achieve perfection. Apprenticed as a toolmaker, he first entered business in 1898 supplying fittings for the cycle and motorcycle trades. He met Charles Riley Garrard who imported small engines and, in 1902, used one of these engines to create the first Norton motorcycle - in essence, a French-built 160cc Clement that was bolted to the downtube of a strengthened bicycle frame. The engine had an automatic inlet valve and low tension ignition, but the transmission was innovative, offering either direct belt drive, or chain drive to a two-speed gearbox sited below the crankcase and from there to the rear wheel by means of a belt. The machine was advertised as the Energette, but only for that year.

Various models were put on the market in 1903 and late in the year a ladies version was added, arising from a request by an agent on behalf of his wife. The result fitted a Clement-Garrard engine to an open frame, transmission being by chain to a two-speed gear and clutch.

Norton then concentrated on the components supply business, but continued to advertise complete machines, no doubt purpose building to specification for anyone who cared to place an order. By 1906 a range existed, mainly using Peugeot engines with direct belt drive; production however, remained minimal.

First to bear the famous name, the 1902 model fitted with a 160cc Clement engine and two-speed gearbox.

A Norton advertisement from late in 1908 using the 'Unapproachable' slogan to promote both single and twin-cylinder models.

MY "UNAPPROACHABLE"

NORTON

"The smoothness & comfort are marvellous."

A Remarkable Performance at the Birmingham Motor Cycle Club Hill-climb. H. Rem Fowler, on his 5 h.p. Twin NORTON, carried off every prize, making FASTEST TIME in the speed test, WINNING THE SLOW CLIMB, and the Medal for the machine showing GREATEST FLEXIBILITY on the hill. NO ADJUSTMENT WHATEVER was permitted between trials.

The 5 h.p. NORTON holds the RECORD for the T. T. Course, I.O.M.

The 5 h.p. NORTON has record petrol consumption Twins, 1908.

NORTON MOTORS are MECHANICALLY and SCIENTIFICALLY CORRECT.

NOTE THE LINES—THEIR SIMPLICITY AND NEATNESS.

5 h.p. TWIN, 50 Guineas   Ready for the Road.   3½ h.p. SINGLE, 40 Guineas

THE NORTON MANUFACTURING CO., LTD., BIRMINGHAM.

The firm's fortunes changed when Rem Fowler won the Multi-Cylinder Race at the first Touring Trophy (TT) in 1907, using a Norton powered by a 690cc Peugeot V-twin engine. This success, highlighted in the company's advertising, brought the marque to the public's attention. Norton went back to Birmingham to continue his design work and the result was the first Norton engine and three models, two twins and a single.

One twin was based firmly on the successful Peugeot, but with improved features, while the other revived the Energette name and was powered by a 274cc Moto Rêve V-twin engine, Norton being the Midland agent for that firm. The single had a 475cc engine and mechanical valves. During 1908 the Nortonette, powered by a 2hp, 241cc Motosacoche single-cylinder engine, appeared briefly, the Energette then taking its name before it too was dropped. That year saw the slogan 'Unapproachable Norton' being used in an advertisement for the first time.

Norton himself was still riding in competition, including the TTs in 1909, 1910 and 1911, debating issues and technical matters with his contemporaries, and designing new models, including one with a two-stroke engine. In his fascination with technical matters he ignored the financial side of running the company. When the inevitable fiscal crisis occurred, he had to be bought out by R T Shelley who retained Norton as joint managing director.

Rem Fowler, after his win in the 1907 TT, with James Norton standing beside him, behind the machine.

The deal put the firm on a sound business footing from which the marque progressed slowly and surely. Change for change's sake was not to be a Norton characteristic - major alterations remained few as the decades rolled by. The single became the mainstay of the business by the end of the Edwardian era, the range condensing to two models, one of 496cc, the other the 634cc Big Four intended for sidecar work. Pedals or footboards were available, but all had direct belt drive and no gearbox other than the option of a three-speed rear hub or expanding engine pulley.

For 1912 the smaller engine was joined by another to introduce the classic 79mmx100mm dimensions and 490cc capacity. The 496cc engine was dropped at the end of the year, while the others ran on in various forms, these listed under a series of model numbers from 1916.

After 1907, success in the TT eluded Norton for years, but in 1912 the company began to make its mark at Brooklands, first Brewster and then Emerson setting new records. In 1913 O'Donovan began using Nortons to set world records at the track. His association with the marque led to the introduction of the Brooklands Special (BS) model, guaranteed to exceed 75mph for the flying kilometre or 70mph for one lap. A certificate was also awarded, although this and the guarantee really only applied to the engine, which had been fitted to a slave frame at the track for its run.

The famous Norton side-valve single whose lines changed little from start to finish. It was built in two capacities.

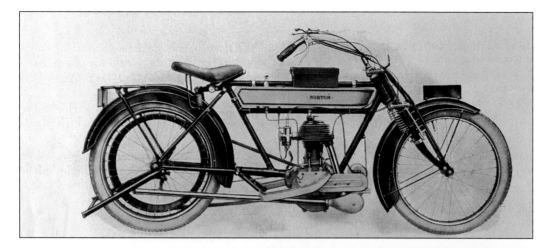

The basic model for 1913 with 490cc engine and direct belt drive to the rear wheel.

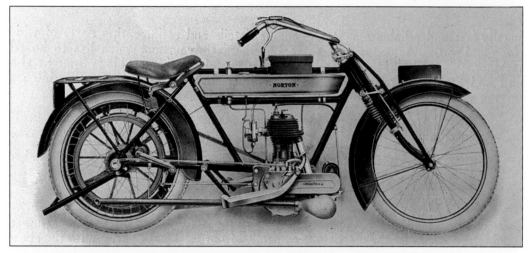

This version for 1913 had its three speeds built into the rear-wheel hub and a handle starter.

The TT Model 9 that had narrow mudguards, footrests rather than boards, and was sold for sporting riding or racing.

In addition to the BS model, there was also the Brooklands Road Special (BRS), which came with mudguards and other road equipment, and whose engine had to do its kilometre at over 70mph and its lap at over 65mph. O'Donovan did much of the testing, being adept at changing engines and at coaxing the best from them out on the concrete.

Then came the Great War. Norton, as a small company, was barely involved in the supply of machines to the services, so normal production continued, some of the 1915 models being equipped with three-speed countershaft gearbox and all-chain drive for the first time, but most retained the direct belt drive and simple construction of old. In 1915 O'Donovan set still more records and in 1916 the Model 16 was launched, the first of a series that ran until 1954. It used the 490cc side-valve engine, three-speed gearbox and all-chain drive. Later, in 1921, would come a Colonial version, the 17C, so the original then became the 16H, 'H' for home.

The range of models was increased by offering alternative specifications such as chain or belt drive. This practice was used to extend the model line-up, and was to continue for many a year. In the 1930s it was extended further by adding a twin-port head and second exhaust system, or by offering other options.

After the war, Norton offered much the same lines as before. The 634cc Big Four Model 1 and 490cc 16H used chain drive, the other three 490cc models, the basic TT Model 9, the BS Model 7 and BRS Model 8 used a belt. It took time for production to get underway but Norton was now an influential firm in the industry, well removed from its prewar standing as only a minor motorcycle manufacturer.

For sidecar work Norton recommended this 634cc Big Four, also listed as the Model 1, for its better pulling power.

Known as 'Old Miracle', this famous machine was used by D.O'Donovan to set many records at Brooklands before, during and after the Great War.

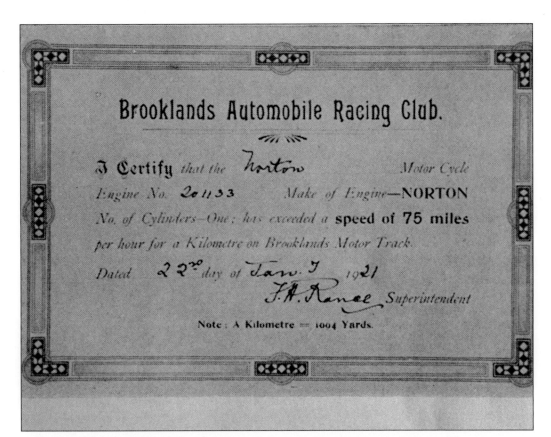

A 1921 Brooklands Special certificate for engine 201133 that exceeded 75mph for the kilometre. The alternative was a lap at over 70mph. The Brooklands Road Special could run 5mph slower.

A 1922 TT Model 9. In BRS form it cost an extra £12 while £22 would get the BS that came with both Binks Rat-Trap and B & B carburettors.

BRACEBRIDGE STREET 1920-1930

In 1920 Norton moved to Bracebridge Street, Birmingham the address it was to use until 1963, and destined to become famous around the world. There was no immediate change to the range itself which did not alter until 1923. However, in March 1922 an overhead-valve (ohv) Norton appeared for the first time, prepared by O'Donovan and ridden by his jockey, Rex Judd, at Brooklands. It was based on the side-valve engine, retained the 79mmx100mm dimensions, had vertical pushrods and plenty of room for cooling air to flow over the head and under the rocker box. The new machine was later raced, unsuccessfully, in the TT, but scored a win in the Ulster Grand Prix.

The ohv Norton duly appeared in the 1923 range as the Model 18, this being the final year for the simple belt-drive Model 9, while the BR and BRS models were dropped. The same year saw them doing better at the TT races with two second places while they won the prestigious Maudes Trophy in the first of these tests of stock machines.

Taken from the 1930 brochure, this drawing included the R.T. Shelley works where Norton parts and many other goods were made.

The home of the unapproachable

Norton

REG. TRADE MARK

**NORTON MOTORS (1926) LTD
BIRMINGHAM - ENGLAND**

Telephones:
Aston Cross 0775-7-8.

Telegrams·
"Nortomo, Birmingham."

Code: ABC 5th Editions.

The belt drive Model 9 was listed to 1923. This one is from 1920 and shows the bare essentials and simplicity of the type.

The Big Four for 1922, by which time it had three speeds, chain drive, kick starter and a full chaincase.

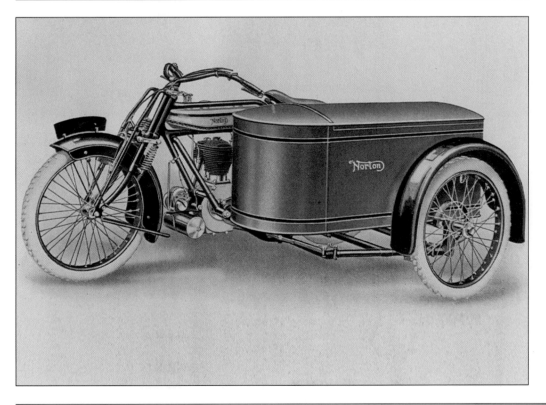

In addition to passenger sidecars, the firm also offered this goods delivery box for an era when motorcycles outnumbered cars.

The next year, 1924, was even better on the competition side with two TT wins, success in several important European races, and the retention of the Maudes Trophy. However, the model range remained as before, basically the side-valve 16H, 17C and Big Four plus the ohv Model 18. There were also a couple of sidecars and the Model 2 - simply a 16H with Colonial touring bars, footboards and balloon tyres.

In April 1925, James Norton died from cancer, aged 56, having kept going through sheer will-power for two long, painful years. He was deeply missed but his name continued to appear on machines that virtually all had upright engines, perhaps symbolic of his nature and standards.

So Norton's road models of the 1920s experienced little change. In 1926 the Model 19 was introduced with a 588cc ohv engine which, when fitted with the optional four-speed gearbox, became the Model 24. In the same way the Model 14 was the Big Four with four speeds. The firm won the Maudes Trophy for the fourth year in succession, and Stanley Woods won the Senior TT riding a works-prepared Model 18, but this was now becoming distinctly long in the tooth.

While the 490cc 16H shared the three-speed gearbox and chain drive of the Big Four, it lacked the chaincase or footboards.

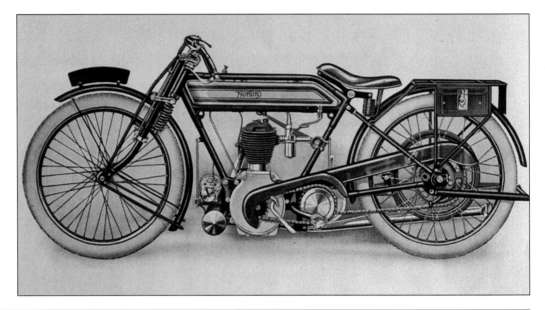

First Norton with an overhead-valve engine was this 490cc Model 18 of 1923 that introduced a new frame and minute front drum brake.

NORTON 18.
Code Word : SPEEDY.

The 490cc overhead-valve engine that kept the classic Norton 79mmx100mm bore and stroke dimensions throughout its long life.

Belt drive for its last year and drum brake signify the 1923 Model 9 TT Norton. Increased traffic ruled out the direct drive.

NORTON NINE T.T.
Code Word: TROPHY.

The range was extended with variations, but most were simply the result of combining engines, gearboxes, frames, forks and cycle parts in different ways. Much of this arose from the difficult postwar trading conditions, to counter which Norton introduced the Model 25, a replica of Wood's TT machine, and the Model 21, an 18 with an improved lubrication system.

For racing, Norton desperately needed something new and Walter Moore, who had joined the firm in 1924 as team manager, was given the task of finding it. The result was the first overhead-camshaft Norton engine and a new cradle frame. The engine was based on the ohv model, but with two bevel pairs and a vertical shaft to drive the camshaft in its housing on top of the cylinder head. A rear-mounted magneto, driven from the crankshaft, replaced the typical front mounting and the result won the 1927 Senior TT.

Brochure front cover for 1923 showing a 16H solo and a Big Four hauling the Family Sidecar carrying mum and child.

Big Four plus De Luxe or Family sidecar, listed as the 'Completely Equipped Norton' for it came with lights and windscreen.

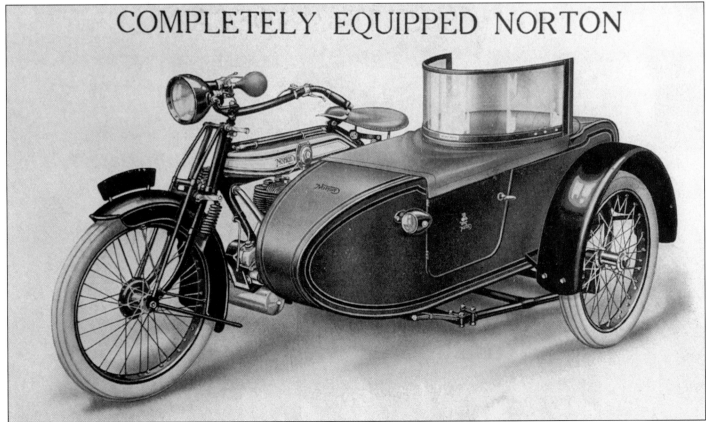

COMPLETELY EQUIPPED NORTON

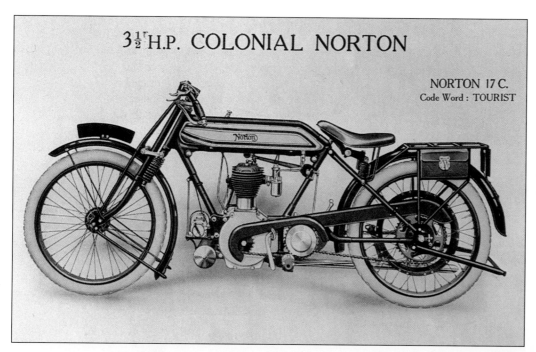

3½ H.P. COLONIAL NORTON

NORTON 17 C.
Code Word : TOURIST

Based on the 16H, the 17C Colonial had more ground clearance and other changes to suit its purpose.

In 1923 Norton offered the 'Dorway' sidecar whose body lifted off and chassis folded to enable it to pass through a 28in opening. Here the body's in the process of removal.

Here the 'Dorway' sidecar has had the body removed and the chassis folded in, keeping the sidecar wheel in line.

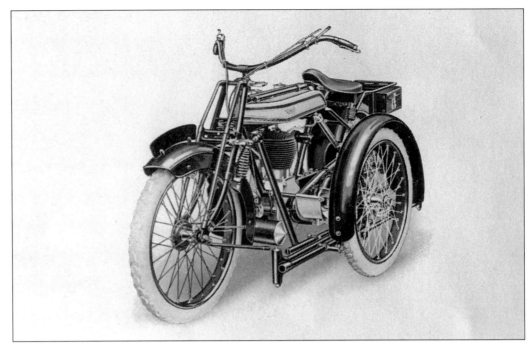

Four speeds were offered by the Model 14 version of the Big Four, with the final drive chain on the right as on this 1926 machine.

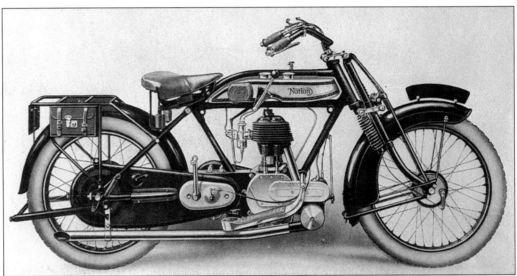

Typical of the flat-track era when Norton adopted the gearbox and chain drive while keeping to its early line; a 16H from 1922.

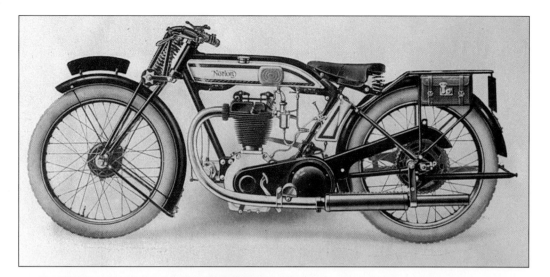

The 1926 version of the Model 18 with drum brakes for both wheels and an improved front fork with centre spring.

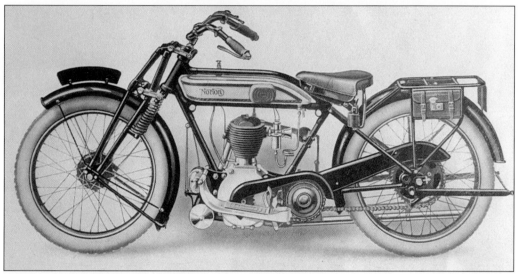

This is the Model 2, effectively a 16H with footboards, but still fitted with the Druid front forks in 1926.

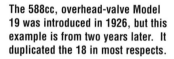

The 588cc, overhead-valve Model 19 was introduced in 1926, but this example is from two years later. It duplicated the 18 in most respects.

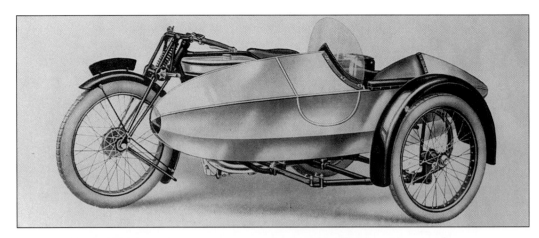

Semi-Sports Touring sidecar for 1926 and modelled in a style that was still in favour many years later.

In this form the 588cc ohv machine had four speeds and was listed as the Model 24. Its year is 1926 and the gearbox the cross-over type.

Wonderful lines of the first Norton camshaft engine, designed by Walter Moore and taken by him to NSU.

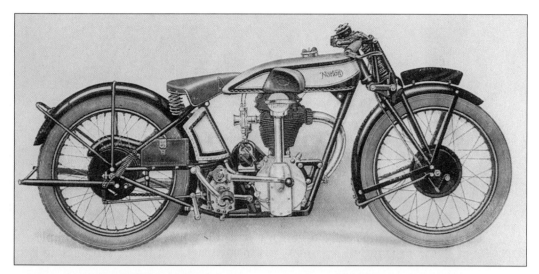

First camshaft model was the 1928 490cc CS1 that had a new cradle frame, rear-mounted magneto and a saddle tank.

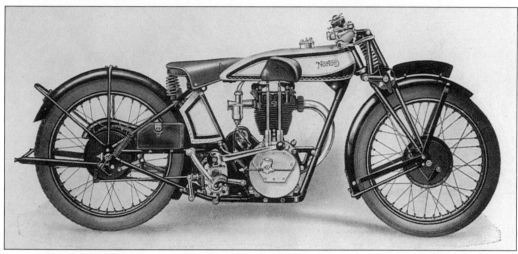

Sharing the frame, magneto position and tank of the CS1 was the 1928 ES2 whose 490cc engine differed a good deal from that of the Model 18.

The dated lines of the 1928 Big Four were not improved by the strange silencer used for that year and the next.

In 1929 Norton introduced two models for the 350cc class, this being the overhead-valve Model JE based on the ES2.

The CJ model had a 348cc overhead camshaft engine much as the CS1 and shared its lighter frame with the JE.

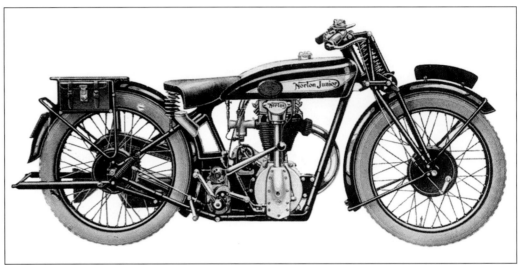

Well restored 1929 CS1 showing off the lines of the Moore engine and the other features of the model.

The 16H may have had a saddle tank in 1930, but it still retained the Druid forks and front magneto.

Front cover of the 1930 brochure featuring a Model 18 rather than the CS1 or ES2.

The cradle frame was used for a new ohv model, the ES2, also with rear magneto mounting. For 1928, both models went on sale to the public, the camshaft machine was listed as the CS1 and fitted with saddle tanks, although the rest of the range kept the flat tank. 1928 also brought a strange, double-barrelled silencer and 1929 saw saddle tanks for the whole range. The same year two 348cc models were added to the stable which acknowledged the appearance of the works riders in that class during 1928. The JE had an ohv engine and the CJ a camshaft one, both fitting into a lighter version of the cradle frame, but otherwise as the ES2 and CS1. However, the early-vintage looks were still there, despite a cast alloy cover over the front-mounted magneto, and the side-valve models still retained the ancient Druid-type front forks.

As shown in the brochure, the 1930 CS1 had the Carroll engine bottom half but retained the Moore top end.

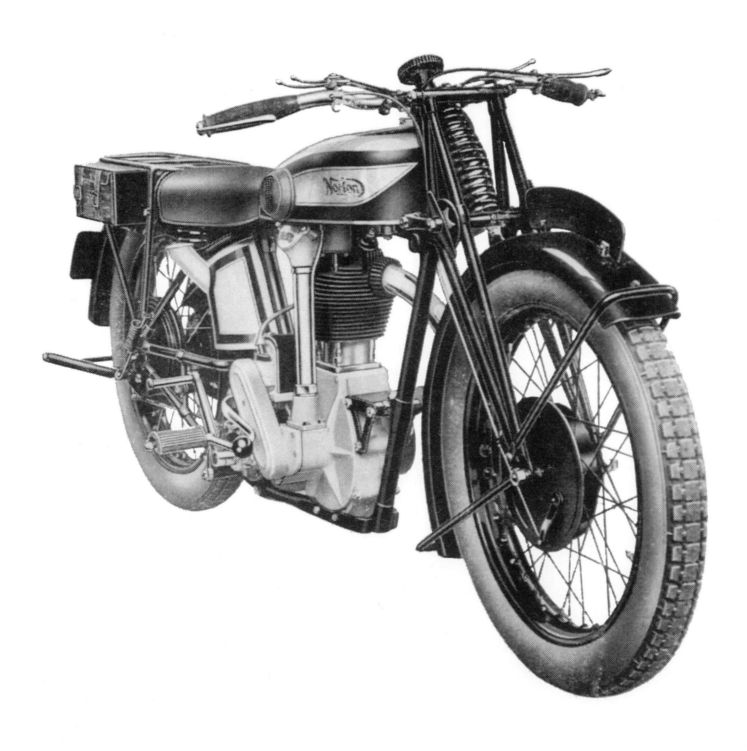

Drive side of the 1930 JE showing the massive cast-alloy primary chaincase, split horizontally.

Twin-port engines were a new trend which Norton followed with this Model 20, based on the 18, its forward magneto hidden by a massive alloy shield.

There was little racing success in 1929, as the result of which Walter Moore left to join NSU in Germany. Joe Craig, who was to become famous as Norton's race director, took over; he was already familiar with the machines, having been racing and winning on Nortons since 1923. He quickly overcame the problems with the works engines and then set to work with Arthur Carroll on the design of a new overhead-camshaft engine.

The prototype was first seen at Olympia late in 1929 and comprised a new crankcase on which sat a Moore top end. That crankcase, with the magneto driven on the timing side and the square, bottom-bevel box, was to become familiar to racing fans from then on. By the time the 1930 season came round the new ohc engine had a revised cambox and the result became known for all time as the Carroll engine.

Norton hovered on the threshold of a great period in its history. However, it took time to develop the Carroll engine so it was not until the Ulster that success came Norton's way in a classic. The 350cc version had no more success, although one won its class in the North West 200.

Meanwhile, the road models lost the double-barrelled silencer but otherwise retained their vintage style, being joined by the Model 20, a twin-port 18, and the 22, a twin-port ES2. Speedway was booming as a sport and in competition with many other firms Norton released its own model, but few were sold, so it soon disappeared from the catalogue.

One of a series of sidecars offered for 1930, ranging from this sports type to the family touring saloon.

The ES2 was offered in twin-port form as the Model 22, seen here in 1930.

By 1930 the ES2 had these lines and in this case had a dynamo mounted on the front of the crankcase.

REVISED SINGLES 1931-1945

Everything changed in 1931. The Norton race team at last came to prominence; Tim Hunt won both the Junior and Senior TTs, Bill Lacey broke the classic hour record late in the year using a camshaft Norton, and the road models took on what was to be their final format. The essentials of the changes were simple. For the side and overhead valve engines the magneto went behind the engine where it was chain- driven from the inlet camshaft; the dynamo was strapped onto the magneto, and dry sump lubrication was adopted with a gear pump in the timing chest. The frames were revised, becoming lower and shorter, a diamond design serving all except the JE, ES2 and the 22. For these, and the CS1 and CJ, there were two versions of the cradle frame, both camshaft engines being of the Carroll type.

By 1931 the CS1 engine had taken on the familiar form it would keep for most of its life on the road and racing track.

Smallest of the overhead-valve models was this 348cc JE in the style used right through the decade although this model was dropped after 1931.

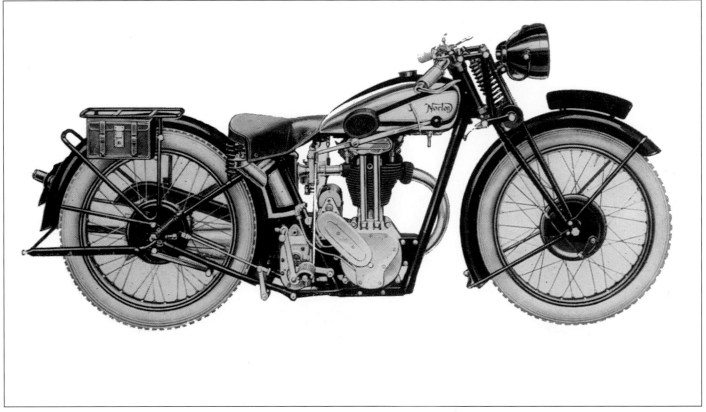

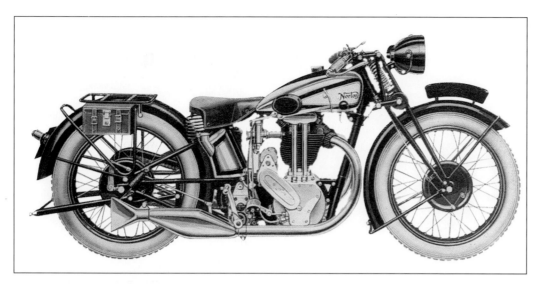

The engine changes of 1931 allowed the twin-port Model 22 to continue, based as before on the ES2.

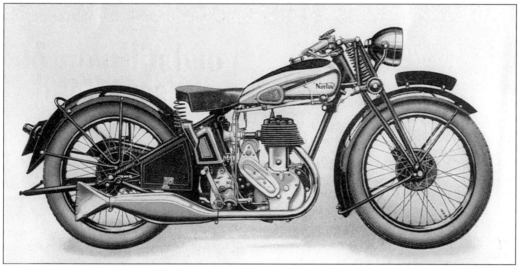

Smaller of the two side-valve models, the 16H had engine changes in 1931 and moved its exhaust to the right for 1932 as here.

New for 1932 were the 348 and 490cc International versions of the camshaft models; this is the larger model.

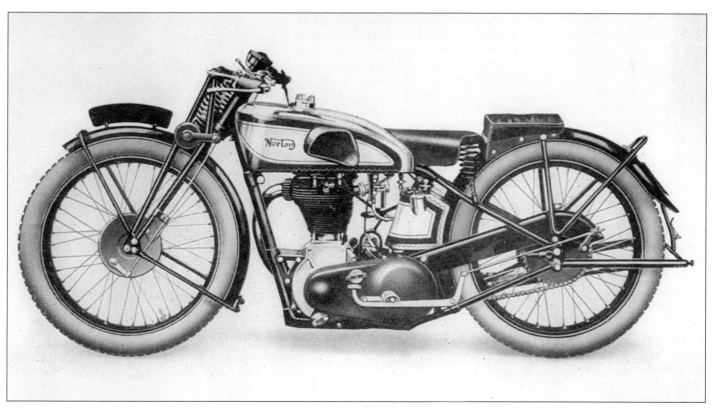

For 1932 the Model 18 kept its exhaust system on the left and still had hand change for the gears.

Typical sports sidecar for the early years of the decade when times were hard and the price everything.

This 348cc Model 50 was new for 1933, along with a twin-port, Model 55 version, to replace the JE.

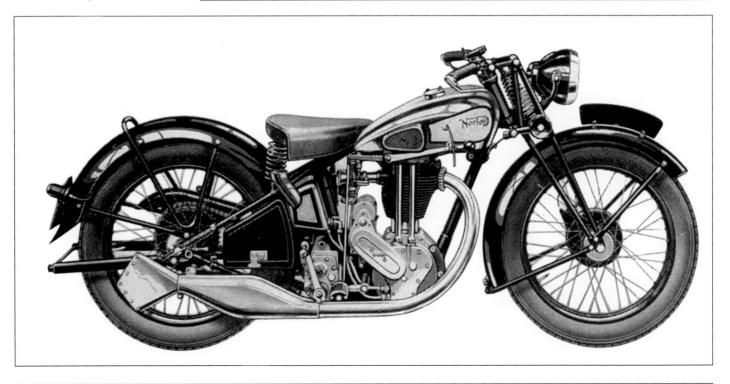

Norton dominated the racing scene for most of the decade, Tim Hunt, Stanley Woods, Jimmy Simpson, Jimmy Guthrie, Wal Handley, Crasher White, Walter Rusk, Freddie Frith and Harold Daniell being the stars who rode the camshaft singles to success in the classic races. Near the end of the period the 350cc Velocette gave them a hard time, as did the 500cc supercharged BMW and Gilera multis in 1938 and 1939. For that last prewar year there was no works Norton team so little success was achieved at the top level.

The standard models progressed steadily through the 1930s. For 1932 the overhead-camshaft International versions of the CJ and CS1 were introduced in 348 and 490cc capacities, these being built in racing trim, although available and usually supplied with road equipment.

The next year saw revised forks on the Inters, the introduction of the 348cc Models 50 and twin-port 55 as smaller versions of the 18, and a change of capacity to 597cc for the 19. An oil-bath primary chaincase came in 1934 when the revised forks became standard on all models, and 1935 brought the Norton four-speed gearbox. That year also saw a trials specification being offered for all models which continued to 1939.

Part of the front cover of the 1933 brochure sheet showing off the joys of owning a Norton.

By 1934 the Model 19 capacity was 597cc and it fitted the oil-bath primary chaincase common to the range that year.

The smaller, 348cc International in 1934. It was always listed as the Model 40, the 490cc version being the Model 30.

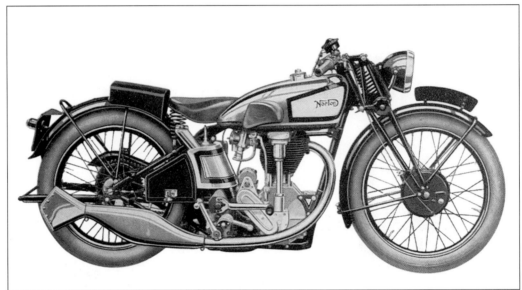

From 1935 any model was said to be available on request in a trials specification. This would be an 18 or 19 and is from 1938, hence the odd silencer.

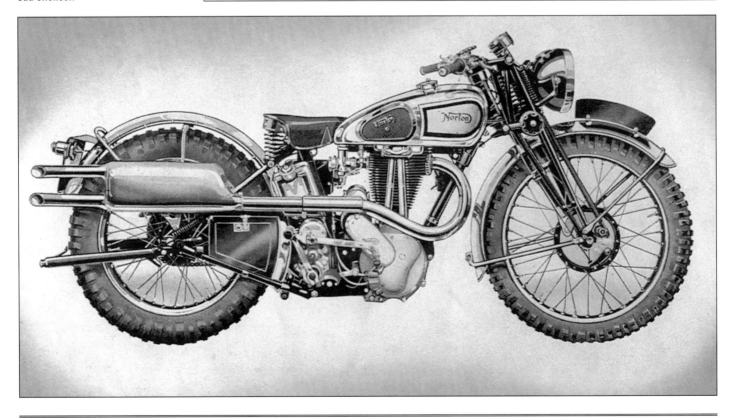

The first year for the four-speed Norton gearbox with foot change was 1935; here it is fitted to an ES2.

Front cover of the 1935 brochure that combined the many racing successes of the firm with its use as a sidecar model.

A series of details from the 1935 brochure.

A couple discuss a Model 18 solo.

Solo rider on a twin-port Model 20 or 55.

The sidecar man and his lady.

An International doing the business!

For 1938 the Inters had the option of a plunger frame while the sv and ohv models had a revised timing chest and a vast, unsightly, silencer. This went for 1939, when the plunger option was extended to the CS1, CJ and ES2, while the Inter became available as the Manx Grand Prix, a pure road racer, as well as available in road form. Not publicised in the catalogues was a 597cc version of the camshaft engine, which was built from around 1935 for road racing or ISDT sidecar work. Not many were built but they were successful.

Norton intended to have revised engines and frames for 1940 but by then the firm was fully occupied in producing large numbers of the 16H in its 1937 form for the services. The motorbikes served well, over 100,000 being built, along with a number of Big Four outfits with a sidecar-wheel drive. There was also a batch of lightweight 350s produced with all-alloy, side-valve engines, but these were lost at Dunkirk.

Touring, or just out for a ride, again a Model 20 or 55.

Mussolini was a motorcycle enthusiast so he would not have missed the chance to inspect the opposition.

International to racing specification for 1938 with a host of options including an all-alloy engine, and many special parts.

The 1938 Model 55 twin-port had one of these strange silencers on each side. They were only used for this one year.

Even the International models, this a 348cc Model 40, had to carry the twin-outlet silencer.

The Model 50 of 1939, reflecting the changes over the decade, including the revised pushrod tubes and rocker enclosure from the previous year.

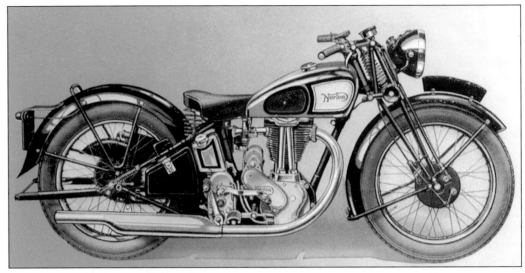

Twin-port Model 20 as shown in 1939; essentially a Model 18 plus the extra exhaust system.

The Big Four continued as the side-car model for 1939, being adapted for service use in the war, while the solo 16H was used in its 1937 form.

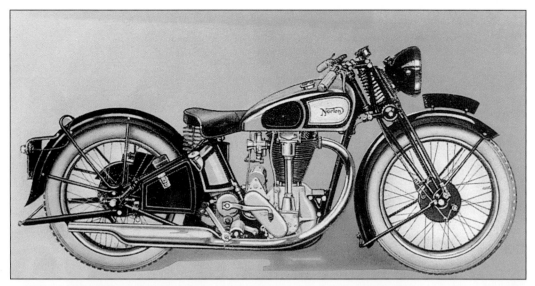

Sports Norton with the camshaft engine in its final 1939 form, for this CS1 and the CJ were not built postwar.

Taken from the brochure announcing the 1946 models, this picture showed how the two Norton side-valve models played their part.

POSTWAR AND TWINS 1946-1958

When the war was over the services sold off their surplus 16Hs and Big Fours, the latter having the sidecar wheel drive cut away for safety reasons, while the firm went back to building civilian models. They began with just the 16H and 18, these being in their 1939 form with girder forks, but using the cradle frame. This rig continued for 1946, but late that year a few racing machines were produced, built solely for competition and sold as Manx Nortons -- the famous name was finally in use. These machines were much as prewar models, using the plunger frame but fitted with Roadholder telescopic forks, which were developed from the prewar works type to include hydraulic damping.

The range was expanded for 1947 with the Manx in 348 and 498cc forms, the International built as a road model in two capacities, the return of the Big Four and the ES2 (the latter with the plunger frame) and trials models in the two sizes. These last were modified road machines, too long and heavy to be competitive, and were dropped in 1948, the year when the Big Four reduced its capacity to 597cc.

Postwar, the 16H went into the cradle frame but kept its girder forks for a year or so.

The Model 18 copied the 16H and, like it, had a minor change to tidy up the gearbox and fitted the 1939-type engine.

The camshaft models returned late in 1946 as the Manx Norton, following on from the prewar machines but with Roadholder forks.

Only the International camshaft road models were listed postwar, offered in the 348cc Model 40 and 490cc Model 30 forms.

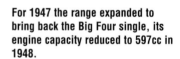

For 1947 the range expanded to bring back the Big Four single, its engine capacity reduced to 597cc in 1948.

Plunger frame and Roadholder forks were standard for the postwar ES2 when it returned in 1947.

The massive 1947 trials model, based on the 18 and listed in 348cc and 490cc sizes despite no Model 50 in the range.

New for 1949 was the Model 7 Dominator 497cc twin that introduced the 'laid-down' gearbox but was otherwise as the ES2.

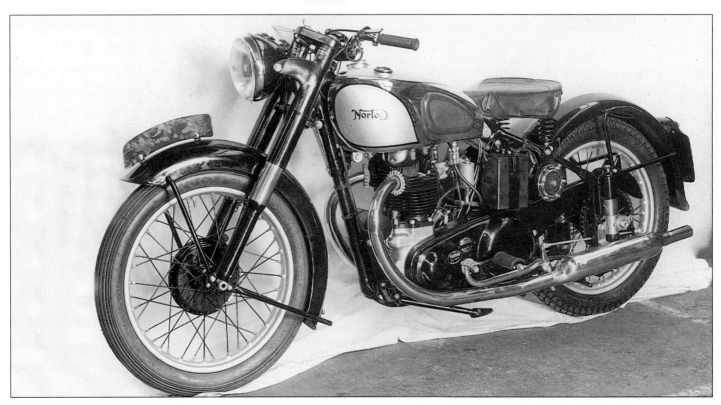

For 1949 Norton added the Model 7 Dominator twin to its range, the engine being so powerful that it was destined to be used for three decades. It was a conventional parallel twin having a single, front-mounted camshaft to lift its overhead valves and an excellent combustion chamber form that enabled it to produce good power. It slotted into the ES2 cycle parts so was always listed with rear suspension, although a rigid example was built. The same year also saw them introduce the purpose-built and tremendously successful 500T trials model.

Norton was back in the racing scene soon after the war, having good seasons in 1947 and 1948, although less so in 1949 by which time the dated plunger frame was well-past its sell-by date. However, Eric Oliver won the sidecar World Championship and Geoff Duke won the Senior Clubman's TT and the Senior Manx GP.

In 1949 the trials 500T appeared, purpose-built for its job with all-alloy engine and short wheelbase.

The 500T gearbox was the prewar type to allow it to squeeze into its allotted space.

Brochure front cover highlighting
the firm's successes and showing
Geoff Duke and the Manx.

Featherbed slimline frame of 1962
showing the elegant simplicity of
the design. Early widelines had the
subframe bolted in place.

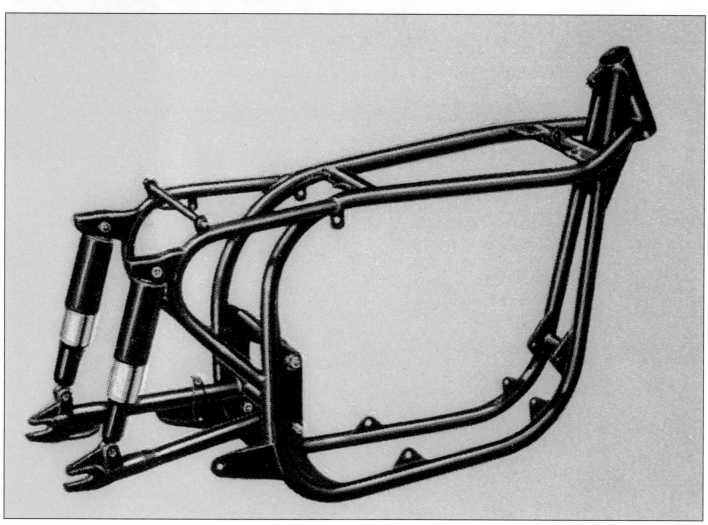

For 1950 and the new decade, there were distinct improvements. The works Nortons appeared in the famous Featherbed frame designed by Rex McCandless, and Geoff Duke became a works rider, while the standard Manx gained the twin overhead-camshaft cylinder head, even if the long-stroke engine dimensions remained the same. Duke dominated the racing season and only tyre problems prevented him from taking the 500cc title. Oliver won the sidecar championship again, and repeated this in 1951 when Duke took both the 350 and 500 titles.

The standard Manx changed over to the Featherbed frame for 1951 and for 1952 the Model 88 Dominator de Luxe was added to the range with the twin-cylinder engine in the Featherbed frame, but as an export-only model. The ES2 and Model 7 were revised into a frame with pivoted-fork rear suspension for 1953, in the case of the twin, this being for sidecar work as the Featherbed was then thought not to be up to this. That year saw the International in the Featherbed frame, using most of the cycle parts from the 88, although the actual frames differed. There was also a one-off side-valve twin, based on the Dominator and aimed at the services market. It had a rigid frame but was not taken up widely.

Racing successes began to decline after Duke moved to Gilera and the light Guzzi proved to have the measure of the heavy Norton in the 350 class. However, Ray Amm won both Junior and Senior TTs while Oliver took his fourth sidecar title. Innovation came in the form of a kneeler machine with full streamlining, nick-named the 'Flying Fish', which although raced only once broke many world records late in 1953. That year was the one when Norton was taken over by Associated Motor Cycles (AMC) which did little to please marque enthusiasts.

A brochure promoting the Dominator twin linking it to racing successes and holiday touring.

This is the twin the customers clamoured for, the Model 88 that combined the engine with the Featherbed frame.

For 1953 the ES2 went into a frame having pivoted-fork rear suspension, but not the Featherbed.

As for the single, the Model 7 twin went to the new frame, and silencer shape, for 1953.

Short-stroke engines finally came to the Manx models in 1954, which proved to be the last year for the old fashioned 16H and Big Four side-valve models, the ohv 18, and the 500T. In their place for 1955 came the 19R and 19S, 597cc ohv singles much as the ES2, one rigid and the other sprung. During 1954 a new works racing design was tried, this having a horizontal, single-cylinder engine and five-speed gearbox. A machine was built to try the engine, which showed promise, but Norton by this time had decided to limit its racing programme and to run just development machines.

At the end of 1955 Joe Craig retired, having been associated with Norton for so many years, and the range for 1956 showed some changes. The 19R and Model 7 went, but the 348cc Model 50 returned as a smaller version of the ES2. The Internationals were no longer listed, but remained available as a special order; the 88 was joined by the 99, an enlarged 596cc version of the twin.

In the major races it was the Italian machines that now dominated, but elsewhere the Manx Norton made up the bulk of the entry in the 350 and 500 classes. Without them, the racing scene would have been very different and competitors owed a great debt to this relatively small firm that provided so much machinery that was so exciting and competitive.

A further sidecar model was offered for 1957, this being the 77 which comprised the 596cc twin engine in the older-style frame as used by the ES2 and 7 models. For 1958, yet another twin was added, the off-road Nomad, built for the USA. It combined the frame from the 77 with a tuned 99 engine fitted with twin carburettors, magneto ignition and an alternator to power the lights. The standard twins changed over to alternator electrics that year and a twin-carburettor option was listed for them.

The year 1958 was the last fling for the International models for they had become outclassed by the BSA Gold Star, were expensive to make and had fallen out of public favour. The 77 and 19S were also dropped as their job of hauling a sidecar was taken over by the 99, thanks to Eric Oliver demonstrating that the Featherbed frame was suitable for sidecar use by taking a stock outfit to 10th place in the TT. This led to a sidecar kit that reduced the fork trail and gave other useful changes.

All-alloy engine and the Featherbed frame for the International in 1953 but the model was not listed for much longer.

Model 19 was built from 1955 and joined the next year by the Model 50. These two and the ES2 were virtually identical larger singles.

For 1956 the larger 596cc Model 99 twin joined the 88, sharing cycle parts and colour.

Manx Norton from around 1956; these models were the backbone of racing and most had regular minor changes to improve them.

JUBILEE AND SS 1959-1970

The twin range was extended in 1959 by the addition of a new model, the 249cc Jubilee, named to celebrate 60 years in business. The machine had a conventional twin-cylinder, overhead-valve engine built in unit with a four-speed gearbox and this assembly went into a composite frame based on a Francis-Barnett design. What set the model apart was the extensive rear enclosure that shrouded much of the rear wheel.

There were radical changes to the singles for 1959 with the 50 and ES2 adopting the Featherbed frame and alternator electrics that brought in many detail alterations and coil ignition. The Manx engine lost its longstanding and characteristic lower bevel box: thanks to a change to the camshaft drive, in place it had adopted the racing AMC gearbox the previous year.

New and smaller 1959 twin was the 249cc Jubilee that also introduced rear enclosure to the marque.

THE ONLY BRITISH 250c.c. TWIN-CYLINDER FOUR-STROKE MOTORCYCLE

Featherbed frame and alternator electrics went onto the ES2 and Model 50 for 1959 along with a forest green finish.

The enclosure went onto the 88 and 99 twins for 1960 to produce the de luxe models with the slimline frame.

Slimline frame and new tank style set off the ES2 and Model 50 from 1961; this is the larger single.

The Navigator was a 349cc version of the small twin but fitted with Roadholder forks and a full-width front brake.

The Jubilee enclosure went on the 88 and 99 twins for 1960 to produce de luxe models. To enable this to be done, the frame main tubes had to be pulled closer around the dualseat nose, the result was soon known as the 'slimline' consequently the early type became the 'wideline'. An 88 Nomad model joined the 99 that year, but both were dropped at the end of the season.

The ES2 and 50 went over to the slimline frame for 1961, also adopting a revised fuel tank style first seen on the Jubilee and taken up by the road twins for 1960. The range of smaller twins was extended by introducing the 349cc Navigator styled like the Jubilee, and offering both models in a standard form without the rear enclosure, the original moving on to become the De Luxe.

Among the heavier twins there was a new, larger model listed at first as the Manxman and intended for the American market. It had the engine stretched out further to 646cc, with twin carburettors and a bright finish to suit its market. Early in 1961 it went on sale in Europe in a standard finish where it was listed simply as the '650'. It was joined by two sports specials, the 88SS and 99SS which were both heavily based on the existing 497 and 596cc models with twin carburettors plus some sporting detail fittings.

Standard versions of the Jubilee and Navigator twins were created in 1961 by dispensing with the rear enclosure, this being the smaller model.

A 650 twin was introduced in the USA in 1961 as the Manxman, but this is the standard UK model produced for the following year.

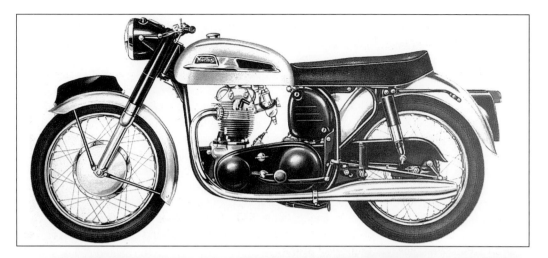

Sports Special or 88SS as for 1963, a model created along with the 99SS in 1961 and fitted with twin carburettors to help it perform.

Taken from the 1962 brochure, this shows the incomparable Mike Hailwood winning the 1961 Senior TT, having run Hocking's MV into the ground.

Manx Norton in its final 1962 form with twin front brake, its engine still clearly related to the first Carroll of 1930.

While the single range was moving to its end with the Manx built from spares, albeit with a dual front brake, the twin machine was still expanding in 1962. All the existing models continued and were joined by a 650 De Luxe with rear enclosure, a 650SS on the lines of the others, and the Atlas. This last had the engine taken out to 745cc, with one carburettor, and a style and finish the same as the other twins.

At the end of 1962 the larger twin range was pruned down to leave just the 88 and 650 in standard and SS builds plus the Atlas. The singles and small twins ran on until 1963 when they were joined by the 383cc Electra which was based on the standard Navigator but with an electric start. The major Norton news that year was the closure of the Bracebridge Street factory and a move to the AMC works at Plumstead.

During 1963 the profounder effects of this amalgamation and move began to show with the appearance of the Atlas scrambler that combined the 745cc Norton engine in an AMC frame fitted with Norton forks and wheels. It was the first of the hybrids.

By the end of 1963 the last Manx had been built and the ES2 and Model 50 were dropped. With them went the de luxe versions of the Jubilee and Navigator, and the 88 and 650 in standard form. New for 1964 was another hybrid, the N15CS 'N', essentially the Atlas Scrambler with a new code.

For one year only, 1962, the 650 was built in De Luxe form with the rear enclosure, after which this was no longer offered.

With the trend to sports models, Norton produced the 650SS for 1962 to complement the smaller machines.

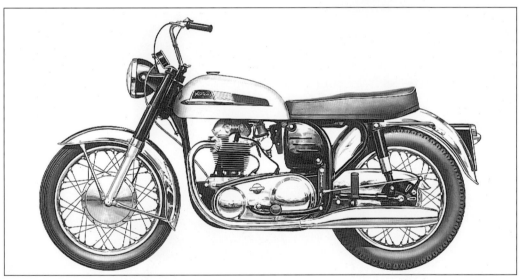

Aimed at the US market, hence the high bars, the 745cc Atlas twin with one carburettor offered 650SS performance in its own style.

The Model 88 in standard form was dropped after 1963, having set roadholding standards for more than a decade.

For 1965 the ES2 and Model 50 returned to the range but in a Mk 2 form that dismayed marque enthusiasts. The machines were really AMC models fitted with Norton tank badges while remaining available as AJS or Matchless models, thus managing to annoy thoroughly all three sets of aficionados in their short, two-year life.

During 1965 a prototype was built using stock parts to house an 800cc twin-cylinder engine having twin, chain-driven, overhead camshafts but this was not taken any further. At the end of the year the Navigator and Electra were dropped, the Jubilee went the same way a year later along with the 88SS.

New ideas were about to take over but during the rest of the decade the 650SS continued on to 1968 and became the single-carburettor Mercury for 1969-70. The off-road N15CS 'N' was joined by the P11 for 1967, this using the Norton 745cc engine in a Matchless G85CS scrambler frame. For 1968 they became the N15CS and P11A, the latter changing name to the Ranger late in the year, but then they were all dropped.

Early in 1963 the 383cc Electra twin joined the other two and featured electric start among its changes.

Final form of the Model 50, dropped after 1963, many of which later donated their frame to a Triton or similar café racer.

The Atlas and the 650SS were produced in a police form, both proving adept at their job.

This 1968 N15CS was derived from the Atlas Scrambler of 1963, the first of the hybrids combining the 745cc Norton engine and an AMC frame.

Prototype 800cc twin built in 1965 with overhead camshafts driven by a chain within the tubes on the right.

The two twins, the 650SS and Atlas as shown in the 1968 brochure.

For 1967 the P11 was created using the 745cc Norton engine and Matchless G85CS scrambler frame to make a nice machine.

In 1968 the off-road P11 twin became the P11A and then the Ranger (as here) before it was dropped.

COMMANDO 1968-1977

n 1967 Norton rethought their twins and came up with the Commando. This combined the well-developed 745cc engine, AMC gearbox and the pivoted-fork of the rear suspension as an assembly and isolated it from the frame, forks, tank and seat. The mounting system was known as Isolastic and relied on close movement control at the three rubber junction points.

In the new model was given a unique style with an inclined engine, a seating position which extended forward to form kneegrips, and a glass fibre seat base extending into a tail section. Seat, tail and the glass fibre petrol tank combined in a fine line and the model went on sale in April 1968.

In this form it was known as the Model 20 Mark III but in March 1969 this was changed to Fastback and two more versions were added. Neither had the tail unit and both were built for the USA street scrambler market. The R had a small tank and high bars but the S had more style thanks to its twin exhaust systems curled round and along the left side of the machine.

Early in 1970 the Fastback and S were joined by the Roadster, which was essentially an S fitted with low level pipes. While the S was soon dropped, the other two then ran on to 1973 with a few minor changes along the way.

First in the Commando line was the Model 20 that became the Fastback and used the 745cc engine.

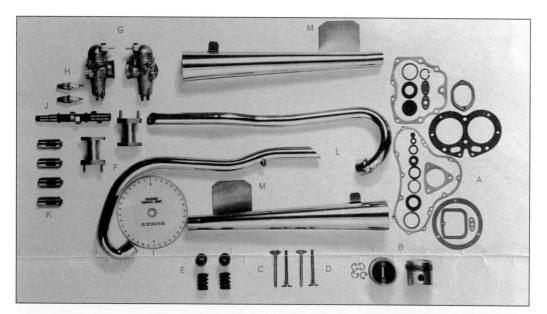

This is the Stage 3 tuning kit devised for the Commando by Paul Dunstall, the leading twin expert, and good for 137mph.

The drum front brake, tubular silencers and timing cover points all indicate a 1969 Fastback in the best of health.

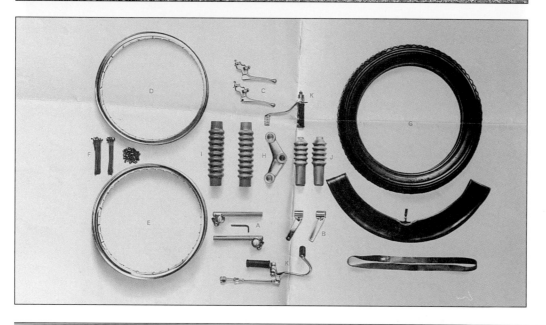

Commando Custom Kit that included alloy rims and, like the tuning kits, never reached the public.

In 1969 the S model joined the
Fastback, its prominent features
being the exhaust systems, slimline
forks and chromed headlamp pro-
tector.

Royal Signals riders with a Fastback
and two model S Commandos about
to be given a thorough work out.

From the S came the Roadster,
essentially the same machine with
low-level exhaust pipes.

Some owners liked the model S style enough to combine it with the larger Commando engine as here. This could have been a factory build.

A year on, so this 1970 Fastback has the reverse-cone silencers but not the slimline forks.

The Roadster of 1971, little altered from its introduction other than for its built-in handlebar switches.

In 1971 they were joined by the Fastback LR (for Long Range) indicating that it had a larger petrol tank. For a few months there was also a Street Scrambler, but more purposeful and successful was the Production Racer built up to 1973. For the custom market, Norton added the Hi-Rider that had high bars and a seat with a massive rear hump. It too ran on with the range.

Problems arose in 1972 when an Interstate model appeared and a performance version of the engine, called the Combat, was made an option. It was just too much for what was, in essence, a 25-year old design, and gave owners and Norton much grief before it was sorted out. It did however mean that the 1973 engines, which were to be the last at 745cc, were good.

Norton worked hard to beef up its engines and early in 1973 enlarged the twin engine for one more time to 829cc. This engine went into the same chassis to produce Roadster, Interstate and Hi-Rider models as before and these continued on to early 1975 with only limited changes. For 1974 they were joined by the John Player Norton, or JPN, a version which came with a fairing as standard. It fitted the stock 829cc engine, but a short-stroke 749cc twin was listed as an option. The name and style of the fairing, tank and seat related to the sponsorship that the firm had enjoyed for its road racing in 1972 and 1973, although unfortunately with limited success.

For 1975 the road models added electric start and moved the gear lever to the left to suit the US market, but by then Norton had been drawn into the general crisis affecting the British motor-cycle industry. Production struggled on into 1977 but then ceased altogether. This brought the police version, built from 1970 and known as the Interpol, to an end.

Production Racer Commando as built for three years and only as a 750. A successful machine and usually finished in yellow.

A Norvil Production Racer, a combination of stock and special parts put together in a competitive package.

The strange Hi-Rider Commando added to the range in 1971 as a chopper-style custom model.

For 1972 this Roadster had the Combat engine and disc front brake as fitted to most machines that year.

The Interstate model joined the Commando range for 1972, its main feature a larger fuel tank, but it too had the revised engine.

The tuned Combat engine brought much trouble to both firm and owners before the problems were sorted out, here in a 1972 Roadster.

Timing side of the 1972 Roadster, complete with disc front brake, slimline forks and reverse-cone silencers.

Fastback as for 1972, still with the unusual seat incorporating the kneegrips, and its base extending as a tail.

In 1973 the Norton twin engine was stretched once more, to 829cc, and installed in three models, this being the Roadster.

The Interstate continued to be fitted with a large petrol tank to enable it to cruise at speed over long distances.

Not standard, a private 850 built in the style of the Fastback Long Range using an Atlas-style fuel tank.

A further Roadster model, this one a modified Mk IIA from 1975 showing the fine lines of the series.

Unexpected, but the Hi-Rider continued to be offered with the larger engine, although sales must have been minimal.

The John Player Norton had its own special style, the fairing, twin headlights and single seat setting it apart from the crowd.

In 1975 the Commando added electric start, disc rear brake, left side gear pedal and improved Isolastic mountings to become the Mk III, as here on the Interstate.

Roadster Mk III with the same changes, including the often ineffective electric starter.

The Commando engine proved highly successful in sidecar motocross when fitted into a Wasp chassis as here.

Police versions of the Commando were built from 1970, this one is from the following year, and known as the Interpol.

ROTARY CLUB 1979-1993

The cessation of production in 1977 was not by any means the end for Norton. During the 1970s the company dabbled with other twins, one the Wulf two-stroke of which only the prototype was ever built, and another the Cosworth, intended for road and racing. While these projects came to nothing, the firm did inherit a rotary, or Wankel, engine project that passed to them from Triumph via BSA.

Small numbers of the rotary-powered machine were built in 1979 for the police, and in 1983 a second version appeared as the Interpol 2, this type also being taken up by the services and the RAC. Finally, in 1987, an interim measure production model was launched as the Classic in a limited edition of 100 with an air-cooled, twin-rotor engine.

The rotary engine type was promoted in 1988 by a return to road racing and during the year the successor to the Classic was launched as the Commander. This had a water-cooled engine and models for both police and public were produced. The smooth power delivery proved popular with riders and the Norton name and reputation enhanced this. In turn, this led to John

Interpol 2 brochure, the police being the first to use the rotary-engined machine that gave a useful feed-back of data.

The air-cooled, twin-rotor engine from the Interpol 2, whose capacity was to be the subject of a technical controversy for years.

The lines of the Interpol 2 were chosen to match those of the BMW R100RS then in police use.

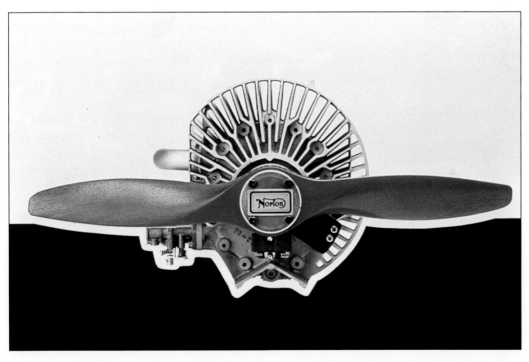

The rotary engine had other applications that included light aircraft, unmanned drones and hovercraft, this NR731 being designed for target drones.

RAC Jambuster, still with Interpol 2 side badge, used to speed through the congestion to rescue members.

Classic was the name chosen for the first rotary-powered Norton to be sold to the public, but only 100 were planned and built.

Engine unit of the Classic was air-cooled and the capacity of the twin chambers given as 588cc, these driving a five-speed gearbox.

Early promotion of the new Norton was by racing this machine in 1988.

Player sponsorship for the race team in 1989, a successful season, and the introduction of the sports F1 model for 1990 finished in the JPS livery.

More was promised for 1991, but the recession and the firm's own financial problems prevented this. In 1992 the F1 Sports replaced the F1, the Commander ran on with a second version fitted with panniers permanently attached, and Steve Hislop won the Senior TT for the firm.

Later that year Norton showed the F2 prototype but by then the company had become enmeshed in a financial morass so production ceased in 1993. Since then, there have been several announcements of a renewal, but unhappily none have come to anything.

For devotees of the marque this is sad, but they can look back to the many glorious years when Norton dominated the race circuits and was held in high regard by all. Many Norton machines continue to be seen on the classic scene, both on the road, the race track and in trials.

Liquid cooling was added to the rotary engine to create the Commander which offered performance without vibration.

Police version of the Commander came with all the extra equipment needed by them to do their job.

By 1989 John Player was once again sponsoring the Norton race effort and so the machines were finished in JP colours.

Leading on from the racing came this sports F1 model in 1990 with its advanced technology and stylish bodywork.

The Commander in its 1991 form complete with matching panniers to suit its long distance travel role.

As shown in its brochure, the F1 Sports with its 95bhp engine, aluminium-alloy frame and ultrasophisticated suspension.

By 1990 the RAC had adopted the police Commander for the rescue service, their two requirements being much the same.

In 1992 Steve Hislop won the Senior TT by just 4.4 seconds after a race-long duel with Carl Fogarty on a Honda.

A paramedic version of the Commander was produced and used in London and other cities for a fast response to emergency calls.

The F2 prototype on show at the NEC late in 1992 but destined not to go into production.

Norton Commander - far removed from James Norton's machines, but technically advanced for its year, just as in the past.

NORTON MODELS

These are arranged by number of cylinders, engine type and years built, plus the model code and capacity.

SINGLES

cc	type	years	code
475	sv	1908-09	
496	sv	1910-12	
634	sv	1910-47	1 (Big Four)
490	sv	1912-23	9 TT
490	sv	1914-22	7 BS
490	sv	1914-22	8 BRS
490	sv	1919-20	16
490	sv	1921-54	16H
490	sv	1921-26	17C
490	sv	1923-32	2
490	ohv	1923-54	18
588	ohv	1926-32	19
588	ohv	1926-30	24
634	sv	1926-30	14
490	ohv	1927-30	21
490	ohv	1927-30	25
490	ohv	1928-30	34
588	ohv	1928-30	44
490	ohv	1928-63	ES2
490	ohc	1928-39	CS1
348	ohv	1929-31	JE
348	ohc	1929-39	CJ
490	ohv	1930-31	22
490	ohv	1930-39	20
490	ohv	1930	Speedway
490	ohc	1932-58	Inter 30
348	ohc	1932-58	Inter 40
348	ohv	1933-39	50
348	ohv	1933-39	55
597	ohv	1933-39	19
348	ohc	1946-63	Manx 40M
498	ohc	1946-63	Manx 30M
597	sv	1948-54	1 (Big Four)
490	ohv	1949-54	500T
597	ohv	1955	19R
597	ohv	1955-58	19S
348	ohv	1956-63	50
348	ohv	1965-66	50 Mk 2
497	ohv	1965-66	ES2 Mk 2

abbreviations

ohc	-	overhead camshaft
ohv	-	overhead valve
sv	-	side valve
t/s	-	two-stroke

TWINS

cc	type	years	code
249	ohv	1959-66	Jubilee
349	ohv	1961-65	Navigator
383	ohv	1963-65	Electra
497	ohv	1949-55	7
497	ohv	1952-63	88
497	sv	1953	military
497	ohv	1960	88 Nomad
497	ohv	1960-62	88 De Luxe
497	ohv	1961-66	88SS
596	ohv	1957-58	77
596	ohv	1956-62	99
596	ohv	1958-60	99 Nomad
596	ohv	1960-62	99 De Luxe
596	ohv	1961-62	99SS
646	ohv	1961-63	650
646	ohv	1962	650 De Luxe
646	ohv	1962-68	650SS
646	ohv	1969-70	Mercury
745	ohv	1962-68	Atlas
745	ohv	1963-64	Atlas MX
745	ohv	1964-67	N15CS'N'
745	ohv	1967	P11
745	ohv	1968	N15CS
745	ohv	1968	P11A
745	ohv	1968	Ranger
745	ohv	1968-73	Commando
747	ohc	1975	Cosworth
800	ohc	1965	Prototype
829	ohv	1973-77	Commando
500	t/s	1973	Wulf
588	rotary	1979-82	Police
588	rotary	1983-93	Interpol 2
588	rotary	1987	Classic
588	rotary	1988-93	Commander
588	rotary	1990-91	F1
588	rotary	1992-93	F1 Sports
588	rotary	1992	F2

abbreviations

ohc	-	overhead camshaft
ohv	-	overhead valve
sv	-	side valve
t/s	-	two-stroke